MARK MATLOCK

WISDOM ON...
GROWING IN CHRIST

ZONDERVAN®

ZONDERVAN.c
AUTHORTRACK
follow your favorite auth

Wisdom On...Growing in Christ
Copyright 2008 by Mark Matlock

Youth Specialties resources, 300 S. Pierce St., El Cajon, CA 92020 are published by Zondervan, 5300 Patterson Ave. SE, Grand Rapids, MI 49530.

ISBN 978-0-310-27932-7

Web site addresses listed in this book were current at the time of publication. Please contact Youth Specialties via e-mail (YS@YouthSpecialties.com) to report URLs that are no longer operational and replacement URLs if available.

Cover design by SharpSeven Design
Interior design by David Conn

Printed in the United States of America

08 09 10 11 12 • 16 15 14 13 12 11 10 9 8 7 6 5 4 3 2 1

To my wife Jade. This is the sixth book in the Wisdom On series, and if anyone has felt the weight of this book it has been her. You are the perfect help to me, as I hope I am to you. I enjoy each day we have to make God known together.

DEDICATION

TABLE OF CONTENTS

I'd like to thank the many people who helped with this volume in the Wisdom On series: Randy Southern, for excellent editing and feedback; Holly Sharp, for the cool covers; Roni Meek and Jay Howver at Youth Specialties; and Brad Taylor, who had to correct my spelling and punctuation. I'd also like to acknowledge my interns, Aaron Giesler, Matt Johnson, Jill Miller, and April Stier, for their conversations with me about wisdom that added to the development of this book. Also to Josh Meares, my research assistant, who helped me get the last few chapters out the door—thank you!

ACKNOWLEDGMENTS

CHAPTER 1

HOW DO I GROW—
AND WHY SHOULD I?

UNDERSTANDING WHAT IT MEANS
TO BE A MATURING CHRISTIAN

I'll be honest. This is a hard book to write.

There's nothing more important than our relationship with God. But after 33 years of being a Christian (it's okay, you can say it: I'm old), I'm still learning how to grow in Christ.

Right now you may be thinking one of two things:

1. Who is this guy to write a book if he still doesn't have it all figured out after 33 years?

OR

2. Phew! This guy's been learning for 33 years, and he still doesn't believe he has it all figured out. Maybe I'm not in such a bad place after all. Maybe I can learn some things from this Mark

Matlock guy that can prevent me from making some of his mistakes.

If you lean more toward the second line of thinking, then join the club. I never trust anyone who believes he has it *all* figured out. In fact, I believe that's almost a certain sign that he's probably missing quite a bit.

I don't have it all figured out—but I've learned a lot in my 33-year walk with Christ. Some of those learning experiences were pleasant, while others were—not so much. (Let's just say I've learned a lot of things the hard way.) My prayer is that by reading about some of the things I've discovered along my journey, you might save yourself some pain and maybe—just maybe— help yourself mature in Christ more quickly.

Someone once said that learning from our mistakes makes us smart, but learning from other people's mistakes makes us wise. So I invite you to learn from my pain so you won't have to experience it yourself!

A NEW CREATION

I love new things. I love the smell of a new car or a freshly painted home with new carpet. I love Christmas and birthdays because I typically receive new clothes. In video game stores, I'm always looking for new experiences.

I like new things, and so does God. Our spiritual journey begins with a new work that God does in our lives. Second Corinthians 5:17 describes it this way: "Therefore, if anyone is in Christ, he is a new creation; the old has gone, the new has come!"

The Bible teaches us that when we put our trust in Jesus, we become a new creation. Spiritually speaking, we aren't what we once were.

But what's changed?

In spiritual terms, we've been born again. But that's a hard concept to get my head around. I look at it as though something mysterious and supernatural has taken place—something that gives me the opportunity to grow spiritually. As a result, I have a chance to do new and incredible things with my life—opportunities that weren't available to me before. I can walk closely with God in a real relationship, I can have healthier relationships with people, and I can feel good about whom God made me to be.

It may be a mysterious process, but when I put this "new me" to the test, I see that I have the ability to make a difference in the world that I never could have made before.

Before I knew Jesus, I was lost. But now I've been rescued, and that allows me to live a new life—a life that looks more and more like the one Jesus lived.

A NEW CITIZENSHIP

In addition to making me a new creation, my relationship with Christ gives me a new citizenship. I may be a dweller of the earth, but my *home* is now in heaven.

It's likely that you were born in a hospital in a particular town. But if you're a follower of Christ, you're not from that town anymore. Now you're from heaven. You no longer belong to the world you were born into: "But our citizenship is in heaven. And we eagerly await a Savior from there, the Lord Jesus Christ" (Philippians 3:20). This means that our new home is a place we've never visited, and that's kind of strange.

I have a friend who's Canadian, but—with the exception of her first two years—she's lived in the United States all her life. When she was in high school, her family decided to move back to Canada. The people in the Canadian province she came from spoke mostly French, but my friend knew very little of the language. So while she was still in the States, she began learning about the place where she was born—including the language and culture of the people living there.

That's kind of what growing in Christ is like. Our citizenship is in heaven, but we've never been there. So Christ came to show us what that kingdom is all about. He told us that while we're away from heaven, we have a responsibility to live as though we're in our true "home."

A NEW CULTURE

Being new creatures and having a new citizenship sets us apart from the rest of the world. It makes us different. We no longer think and act like everyone else does. We belong to a different culture. And our new culture encourages us to be good and loving toward others and to do what is right.

While something mysterious and supernatural has taken place inside our lives, which is solely the work of God, the Bible also talks about our need to actively think and live differently because we are new. This new way of thinking and living is what we'll be discussing in this book because God's Word makes it clear that we are willful participants in this aspect of our new lives.

Look at Paul's words in Romans 12:1-2.

Therefore, I urge you, brothers, in view of God's mercy, to offer your bodies as living sacrifices, holy and pleasing to God—this is your spiritual act of worship. Do not conform any longer to the pattern of this world, but be transformed by the renewing of your mind. Then you will be able to test and approve what God's will is—his good, pleasing, and perfect will.

Notice two words in this passage: *conform* and *transform*. Both refer to the process of being formed, but they have distinctly different meanings. We're told not to be formed in one way and to *be* formed in another. What's the difference?

When I was in third grade, the first installment of the movie epic *Star Wars* came out. Immediately after seeing the movie, my friends and I put away our cowboy guns and our bows and arrows, and we picked up blasters and light sabers instead. No more cowboys and Indians for us; we were playing Jedi and Sith.

I remember receiving a Star Wars Play-Doh set for my eighth birthday. I was very excited. Play-Doh came in only three colors at that time: red, yellow, and blue. So I'd take out a wad of yellow Play-Doh, cram it into the Chewbacca mold, and clamp it down. When I opened it, what popped out was not Chewbacca, but a piece of yellow Play-Doh that had conformed to the "pattern" of Chewbacca. It was still yellow Play-Doh; it was just molded in the image of Chewbacca.

Conform means "to be or become similar in form, nature, or character." And I don't know about you, but I'm happy that God tells us *not* to be conformed. I don't like conforming to anything—

especially the pattern or "mold" of this world.

That refusal to conform raises several interesting questions, one of which Paul poses in Colossians 2:20: "Since you died with Christ to the basic principles of this world, why, as though you still belonged to it, do you submit to its rules?"

Following the "patterns of the world" and living by the rules of our "old" culture can lead to a real mess for Christians. In order to avoid such mistakes, though, we have to know what those patterns and rules are. Fortunately, God's given us some unmistakable clues in his Word:

> Do not love the world or anything in the world. If anyone loves the world, the love of the Father is not in him. For everything in the world—the cravings of sinful man, the lust of

his eyes and the boasting of what he has and does—comes not from the Father but from the world. The world and its desires pass away, but the man who does the will of God lives forever. (1 John 2:15-17)

Based on this passage, we can identify three patterns to avoid.

1. THE PATTERNS OF PLEASURE ("THE CRAVINGS OF SINFUL MAN")

In the days of the New Testament writers, the concept of doing what was pleasing to the body was referred to as "hedonism." The focus of hedonism was to satisfy the desires of the body, "the cravings of sinful man."

Of course, some cravings—or impulses—are natural. For example,

• If you've stayed up late, then you'll feel the impulse to sleep.

• If you're hungry, then you'll feel the impulse to eat.

• If you're attracted to someone of the opposite sex, then you'll feel impulses to get to know the person better.

• If it's cold outside, then you'll feel an impulse to seek shelter and find warmth.

Impulses alone aren't evil. However, if we allow our cravings to dictate our actions, then we'll develop some unhealthy—even destructive—patterns in life.

Consider how the following impulses, when distorted, can cause us pain and suffering.

• The desire for food, when distorted, leads to gluttony, obesity, and other eating disorders.

- The desire for sleep, when distorted, leads to laziness.

- The desire to eliminate pain, when distorted, leads to substance abuse.

- The desire for instant gratification, when distorted, leads to cheating, theft, and gambling.

- The desire for sexual fulfillment, when distorted, leads to premarital sex and adultery.

- The desire to escape from difficult reality, when distorted, leads to too much music, entertainment, video games, and Web surfing.

- The desire to preserve one's self, when distorted, leads to fighting, gossip, backstabbing, cheating, and rebellion against authority.

God calls us to experience something more than slavery to our physical desires. As followers of Christ, we don't live to seek our own pleasure. Instead, we live to please God.

THINK ABOUT IT

· What are some impulses that you feel but choose not to act on because you know it wouldn't be right?

· What are some ways you live to please yourself?

· What are some ways you try to please God?

★ · Are there impulses in your life that you can't seem to control? If so, what specific steps can you take to get the help you need?

2. THE PATTERNS OF POSSESSIONS ("THE LUST OF HIS EYES")

The lust of the eyes, as John describes it, refers to our desire for things. In the Ten Commandments, it's called *coveting*. Imagine you're out shopping one day, and you see an item that you just have to have. You can't get it out of your mind. You'd do just about anything to get it. This is a prime example of lust of the eyes.

In relationships, we talk about guys "lusting" after girls (and vice versa). That's another "possession" problem. When a guy lusts after a girl, he sees her as an object rather than a person. There's a huge difference between love and lust!

I once saw a bumper sticker that sums up the lust-of-the-eyes mindset. It read "He who dies with the most toys, wins!"

That kind of lust isn't confined to just inanimate objects, either. In other words, the more you can get, the better off you'll be. The shortsighted nature of that philosophy inspired some wise person to come up with his own bumper sticker slogan: "He who dies with the most toys, still dies!"

God isn't opposed to our having nice things, but he wants us to pursue true riches, which aren't found on this earth. Look at Jesus' words in Matthew 6:19-21:

> Do not store up for yourselves treasures on earth, where moth and rust destroy, and where thieves break in and steal. But store up for yourselves treasures in heaven, where moth and rust do not destroy, and where thieves do not break in and steal. For where your treasure is, there your heart will be also.

According to Jesus, there are two types of riches. Consider how they differ:

Treasures on Earth

1. They can be enjoyed for 70 years or so while we're alive on earth.

2. They can be ruined and destroyed.

3. They can be stolen or taken away.

4. Jesus tells us not to pursue them.

Treasures in Heaven

1. We have to wait 70 years or so to enjoy them—but they last for eternity.

2. They can't be ruined or destroyed.

3. They can't be stolen or taken away.

4. Jesus tells us to pursue them.

Traces of heavenly treasure can be found in our relationships with others. When I was younger, my friend and I each gave up our savings so another friend, who had no money, could go to summer camp with us. During that week at camp, our friend committed his life to Christ. Eternal riches? Yep. And they were better than the junk we would have spent our money on.

How can you use your possessions to provide for others instead of for yourself? (For more ideas on this topic, check out my book *Wisdom On...Time and Money*.)

THINK ABOUT IT

Go to almost any store, and you can probably find something you'd really like to have. The list of things that people want to accumulate is virtually endless.

· Can you add any items to the following list of things people "lust" for?

Cars

Entertainment systems

27

Cool clothes

Video games

Skateboard equipment

Athletic gear

Jewelry

✗· What are some things you lust for?

· How much stuff do you have that you once thought was important but no longer use?

✗· How could you live so you store up treasure in heaven instead of on earth?

3. THE PATTERNS OF POSITION ("THE BOASTING OF WHAT HE HAS AND DOES")

When my son Dax was getting ready to enter middle school, he started to notice how things were changing all around him. Before he left for school one morning, he crawled onto my bed. I could tell Dax was troubled, so I asked him what was wrong. "It seems like the kids at school are becoming popular in the way that people are popular in the movies and on television," he told me.

My son was beginning to see the world's "pattern of position" emerge. All of a sudden, what you wear, how you look, how much money you have, and what activities you're involved in go a long way toward determining how you're treated. Dax was sad to see those changes. I am, too. The world judges us by standards that few of us can meet. And the end result is that many people often feel left out.

THINK ABOUT IT

· Describe how the world might judge the social position of a person based on the following characteristics:

Skin color

Nationality

Education (how many years of school)

Wealth

Home address

Looks (besides skin color)

Age

Accomplishments

Talent

Our world tells us that we need to meet certain standards in order for our lives to matter. If we don't meet these standards, then we won't enjoy the status that many other people enjoy.

· Write down your thoughts as to why students might believe they can improve their status through the following:

Getting involved in certain highly esteemed activities such as sports or cheerleading

Choosing a high-paying occupation

Being consumed with getting good grades

Hanging out with the popular crowd

Doing stupid things like taking drugs

Sleeping around to get the "right" guy or girl

· What are the dangers of seeking status in the world's way?

God asks us not to conform to the principles of this world, but to be "transformed." Let's look at what that means.

TRANSFORMERS

Maybe you're familiar with the special effect called "morphing." It's used frequently in movies, music videos, and commercials. With modern technology, you can even do some morphing effects on your home computer. But when I was a kid, you could only see them in professional productions.

I remember an Exxon commercial that used the morphing effect. It showed a car (filled with Exxon gasoline) driving on a road. Then, right before our eyes, the car liquefied and stretched and became a tiger running down the road. The results were simply amazing. The commercial showed a transformation, a metamorphosis. One thing (a car) turned into a completely different thing (a tiger). What it had been before, it no longer was. That's transformation.

No matter what we are now—or what we've been in the past—God gives us the opportunity to become something entirely new: To change from a nasty, earthbound caterpillar into a beautiful butterfly that can rise to limitless heights. This transformation comes from the "renewing of [our] mind." In other words, after we've experienced the supernatural part that only God can do, we're given an active part in our transformation by following new ways of thinking.

Jesus was the most original thinker who ever lived. He didn't live like the rest of the world. He broke all kinds of social rules—worldly patterns—because he didn't live like he belonged on the earth. Instead, he represented his Father and the place we call our true home. That's what Jesus calls us to do, too.

In Luke 2:52 we find the only verse that links Jesus' childhood to his adulthood: "And Jesus grew in wisdom and stature, and in favor with God and men." That's it! That's all we know about Jesus' puberty, his teenage years, everything that occurs until he begins his ministry at around 30 years of age. But this is an important verse because it describes how Jesus grew and matured—and how we can do the same.

From this short passage, we see that Jesus grew in four areas of life. We see that he grew socially in his relationships with other people. We see that he grew spiritually in his relationship with God. We see that he grew physically. We'll talk a little bit about some of those items, but we really want to focus on the fourth area of growth—wisdom.

Jesus grew in wisdom, which I believe is the ability to see life as God does and not as the world does. When we talk about the "renewing of our mind" that leads to transformation, I believe it's wisdom that we're after. So let's see what it takes to grow in this area of our lives.

TWO KINDS OF WISDOM

Wisdom in the Hebrew language is a word pronounced "hokma," which means "skill at living life." If you think of someone whom you consider to be wise, then you'd probably say that, for the most part, this person has learned to live life well.

Jesus is the ultimate example of living well. After all, he was perfect in everything he did. Of course, not everyone sees it that way. Some people say Jesus didn't hang out with the right people because he preferred the company of common people like fishermen. He spent time with drunkards, prostitutes, and those suffering nasty diseases. Jesus was killed for doing nothing wrong; and when he died, he had no earthly possessions. Some people might question whether he really knew how to "live life well."

According to the world's system of living, you have to have money, fame, power, beauty, talent, and more in order to be considered "skilled" at living life. What's more, the world's wisdom says, "Look out for yourself if you want to live life well." However, Jesus says you can't be great in his kingdom unless you serve others.

Since these two statements about wisdom conflict with each other, we must choose between them. So whose wisdom will we align ourselves with—the world's or the Savior of the world's?

The New Testament writer James talked about this dilemma in chapter 3 of his book:

> Who is wise and understanding among you? Let him show it by his good life, by deeds done in the humility that comes from wisdom. But if you harbor bitter envy and selfish ambition in your hearts, do not boast about it or deny the truth. Such "wisdom" does not come down from heaven but is earthly, unspiritual, of the devil. For where you have envy and selfish ambition, there you find disorder and every evil practice. (James 3:13-16)

My parents' house is on a septic system, which means there's an underground tank that holds the toilet water after you flush. Periodically, that tank has to be emptied. But on one occasion, we filled the tank more quickly than normal. I remember it clearly because I was taking a shower when it happened. As I was cleaning myself—and enjoying the wonderful feeling of warm water falling on my face—I suddenly smelled something really bad. When I looked down, I discovered the septic tank had backed up, and I was ankle deep in sewage! Gross!

There is wisdom—like sewage—that comes from below. And then there's wisdom that comes from above, like the pure water that helped me clean my body. Let's look again at James 3:

> But the wisdom that comes from heaven is first of all pure; then peace-loving, considerate, submissive, full of mercy and good fruit, impartial and sincere. Peacemakers who

sow in peace raise a harvest of righteousness. (James 3:17-18)

Wisdom that comes from below is characterized by selfishness and envy. It's unspiritual, and it leads to every kind of problem and evil practice. Heavenly wisdom, however, is much different. It's pure, peace-loving, considerate, submissive, full of mercy and good fruit, impartial, and sincere. Which type of wisdom do you want to follow?

The book of Proverbs tells us the fear of God is the beginning of wisdom—real wisdom. If we don't acknowledge God in our lives, then we won't find true wisdom. But how can we align ourselves with God? How do we relate to others? Read on!

CHAPTER 2

IN THE WORLD, NOT OF THE WORLD

HOW TO LIVE LIKE AN ALIEN

If you watch a lot of movies and TV shows, then you've probably seen more than a few alien plot lines. Usually, stories about aliens go in one of two directions.

On the one hand, there are the "bad alien" story lines. They can be found on both the big screen (*Independence Day*) and the small (*V, The X Files*, and countless other sci-fi shows). And their plots typically go something like this: The aliens land, and at first everyone's curious about—and a little frightened of—the visitors. The aliens, who seem to be friendly, offer to help humankind through their advanced understanding of science and medicine. But then some human goes someplace she shouldn't, and she witnesses something that reveals the true nature and intent of the aliens. Turns out, they came to Earth to harvest human beings for food—or they simply came to destroy the human race.

On the other hand, there are "good alien" stories like *E.T.: The Extra-Terrestrial, Men in Black, Mork & Mindy,* the *Superman* movies, and *Smallville.* (Yep, Superman is actually an alien from the planet Krypton.) The aliens in these stories are often alone, stranded on Earth, friendly, and seeking to work with humankind. They try to fit in, and they work to benefit the world around them.

As believers in Christ, we are considered aliens. The apostle Peter makes that clear:

> Dear friends, I urge you, as aliens and strangers in the world, to abstain from sinful desires, which war against your soul. Live such good lives among the pagans that, though they accuse you of doing

wrong, they may see your good deeds and glorify God on the day he visits us. (1 Peter 2:11-12)

As Christians, we are living in a place (the world) that's foreign to us. Our true home (heaven) is nothing like this planet on which we dwell. This world is simply a temporary place for us to reside until we see Jesus again: "But our citizenship is in heaven. And we eagerly await a Savior from there, the Lord Jesus Christ" (Philippians 3:20).

That raises an important question: If we're from somewhere else, then what are we supposed to do while we're here on earth? How should we live?

In Chapter 1, we talked about not conforming to this world, but being transformed. Sadly, many Christians have chosen to settle for a compromise—a type of "Christian conformity" that isn't true godly transformation, but it seems better than complete conformity to the world's patterns. In reality, such compromise creates a very bland and uninteresting Christian life—a life that's actually offensive to God.

I've identified three types of "compromising Christians." Let's take a look at each of them.

THE SECLUDED CHRISTIAN

A secluded Christian tries to avoid the world at all costs. He has very few, if any, non-Christian friends. He reads only Christian books and listens to only Christian music. He's afraid of being influenced by the world, so he avoids it at all costs.

The problem with this approach is that Christians are called to follow Christ's example, and Jesus didn't avoid the world at all. In fact, Jesus associated with sinners so much that the religious leaders condemned him for doing so: "The Son of Man came eating and drinking, and they say, 'Here is a glutton and a drunkard, a friend of tax collectors and "sinners."' But wisdom is proved right by her actions" (Matthew 11:19).

Secluded Christians (consciously or subconsciously) pass judgment on the people around them, and they deem non-Christians unworthy of their interaction and friendship. But Jesus showed love—not judgment—to sinners:

> As for the person who hears my words but does not keep them, I do not judge him. For I did not come to judge the world, but to save it. There is a judge for the one who rejects me and does not accept my words; that very word which I spoke will condemn him at the last day. (John 12:47-48)

While the secluded life may seem like a safe option, it really causes Christians to miss opportunities to be used by God. You see, God wants us to reflect his love to a hurting world. We can't do that from deep inside a bunker.

> [Jesus said:] "You are the salt of the earth. But if the salt loses its saltiness, how can it be made salty again? It is no longer good for anything, except to be thrown out and trampled by men. You are the light of the world. A city on a hill cannot be hidden. Neither do people light a lamp and put it under a bowl. Instead they put it on its stand, and it gives light to everyone in the house. In the same way, let your light shine before men, that they may see your good deeds and praise your Father in heaven." (Matthew 5:13-16)

God has called us to be salt and light in the world—to give life flavor and to show people the way to go. We can't do these things in seclusion. Salt is worthless if it never leaves the shaker, and a light does no good if it's hidden away. In the same way, we can serve as God's salt and light when we're actively involved in the world.

If you're serious about growing in Christ and following his example, then you can't seclude yourself from the world. Let go of any judgmental attitudes you have toward people who don't follow God. Make an effort to really get to know such people, rather than instinctively pushing them away and closing yourself off from them. Try to understand where they're coming from and why they believe as they do—even if you feel their beliefs are wrong.

Furthermore, you don't have to be afraid of the world or of those who follow its ways. While you don't want to put yourself into situations that can cause you harm—or cause you to be influenced beyond what you're capable of handling—you also need to realize that we (as Christians) are put on this earth to offer hope and help to those who don't know God.

THE WORLDLY CHRISTIAN

The worldly Christian is one who enjoys the things the world has to offer, while at the same time she also tries to enjoy the benefits of the Christian life. In other words, the worldly Christian desires to be Christlike, but she is unwilling to give up the things of this world.

Jesus was speaking to the worldly Christian when he said: "For whoever wants to save his life will lose it, but whoever loses his life for me will find it. What good will it be for a man if he gains the whole world, yet forfeits his soul? Or what can a man give in exchange for his soul?" (Matthew 16:25-26).

Christians who try to save their lives on earth (by fully enjoying what the world offers) will pay a tremendous price for their efforts—eventually. The fact is that following Christ always costs us something, at least from the world's point of view. For example, I was a virgin when I got married. Many of my friends didn't share my priorities when it came to virginity. They couldn't understand why I wanted to limit my sexual experience to one woman.

I've heard several friends say they won't let being a Christian get in the way of having fun. What they don't realize is that following Christ isn't about losing life experiences—it's about finding life *through* losing. Sure, I may have lost out on some opportunities with girls because I chose to follow God's plan for sex and marriage. But what I *found* was a great reward in my character and in my relationship with the woman I married. What's more, now some 20 years later, I've had numerous friends tell me they wish they'd also saved sex for marriage.

Worldly Christians want the best of both worlds. Yet what they end up with is a double dose of disappointment. They discover—usually too late—that the world's pleasures are fleeting and often come with a high price. And by pursuing worldly pleasure, they miss out on the wonder and depth of a fully committed relationship with Christ.

God has the best in store for us, but we have to give up the world's system of living in order to find it: "Since, then, you have been raised with Christ, set your hearts on things above, where Christ is seated at the right hand of God. Set your minds on things above, not on earthly things" (Colossians 3:1-2).

THE LEGALISTIC CHRISTIAN

The legalistic Christian believes that living the Christian life is best accomplished by following a specific set of rules. The more do's and don'ts he follows, the more spiritual he feels.

And while there's no question that rules tend to make things clear, the Bible tells us that Christ came to set us free and give us life. Jesus doesn't weigh us down with a giant rule book. He knows that if we're bound by a bunch of rules, then we'll probably spend more time trying to understand the rules than doing what he wants us to do.

That's a tough idea for legalistic Christians to understand. After all, rules give them a sense of identity, not to mention a convenient gauge for measuring their own spirituality—as well as the spirituality of others.

That's why the apostle Paul wrote—

> Since you died with Christ to the
> basic principles of this world, why,
> as though you still belonged to it,
> do you submit to its rules: "Do
> not handle! Do not taste! Do not
> touch!"? These are all destined to
> perish with use, because they are
> based on human commands and
> teachings. Such regulations indeed
> have an appearance of wisdom, with
> their self-imposed worship, their false
> humility and their harsh treatment
> of the body, but they lack any value
> in restraining sensual indulgence.
> (Colossians 2:20-23)

Rather than spending your time and
energy trying to figure out what you
can and can't do in this life, consider
what God *wants* you to do. In order
to answer that question, you have to
go beyond mere rules—rules that, as

Paul says, lack any value in restraining sensual indulgence.

A better solution is to approach your earthly life as someone who represents heaven—a beloved child of God who will be welcomed into his kingdom someday. That's not to say there aren't biblical guidelines for God's representatives. The Bible is full of instructions designed to help us complete his work and enjoy life to the fullest.

Consider the following passages and then, below each one, write what God wants us to do or to refrain from doing.

It is God's will that you should be sanctified: that you should avoid sexual immorality. (1 Thessalonians 4:3)

Be imitators of God, therefore, as dearly loved children and live a life of love, just as Christ loved us and gave himself up for us as a fragrant offering and sacrifice to God. (Ephesians 5:1-2)

But among you there must not be even a hint of sexual immorality, or of any kind of impurity, or of greed, because these are improper for God's holy people. Nor should there be obscenity, foolish talk or coarse joking, which are out of place, but rather thanksgiving. (Ephesians 5:3-4)

[The Lord said:] "Do not steal. Do not lie. Do not deceive one another." (Leviticus 19:11)

Children, obey your parents in the Lord, for this is right. "Honor your father and mother"—which is the first commandment with a promise— "that it may go well with you and that you may enjoy long life on the earth." (Ephesians 6:1-3)

You'll notice that Scripture is extremely specific in some areas and less specific in others. That's because God never intended for his Word to be used as a rule book. It's actually more of an instruction manual, full of practical tips on how to please God and how to make the most of what he's given to us.

But that's not enough for the legalistic Christian. He wants God's Word to offer definitive answers to every hot-button topic, and he's not above taking Bible passages out of context in order to make it do so.

However, there are certain questions the Bible just doesn't answer. Here are a few of them:

- What's the proper age for someone to start dating?
- Whom should I date?
- What limits should I set for myself when it comes to dating?
- Is dancing wrong?
- Is smoking wrong?

- Should I be a vegetarian?
- Is it okay to see an R-rated movie?
- For whom should I vote?

The legalistic Christian will have a very specific answer for each of those questions, even if he doesn't have specific biblical support for his opinions.

Later in the book, we'll talk about doing what's right because it's an important topic to consider as we seek to grow in Christ. But living according to a bunch of rules is *not* what God had in mind for us Christians.

Think about this: Legalistic Christians often lose out on the joy of fellowship in their relationships because they're so concerned about holding themselves— and others—to "the rules." And many legalistic Christians have lost—or never even experienced—the joy of their salvation because they're so caught up with trying to follow all of the rules. In a sense, they're working to keep— or earn—their salvation, instead of enjoying it as the incredibly free gift that Christ offers to us all.

> The Lord says: "These people come near to me with their mouth and honor me with their lips, but their hearts are far from me. Their worship of me is made up only of rules taught by men." (Isaiah 29:13)

This passage scares me. The idea of believing that I'm doing everything right when, in reality, I'm ignoring God's will and drifting further and further from him forces me to keep my legalistic tendencies in check. Growing in Christ means we chase after God's heart, not look for the next rule or regulation to follow.

So which one are you? Do you see yourself in any of these three descriptions? Have you been molded into a secluded, worldly, or legalistic Christian? Do you struggle with certain tendencies that prevent you from growing in Christ? If so, then it's time to be transformed and experience something more. Here's a better understanding of how we should live.

THE CHRISTIAN AMBASSADOR

In New Testament times, Corinth was a coastal city with many ports that attracted traders from all over the world. And like many coastal cities, Corinth was home to many extreme lifestyles and false religious beliefs. The setting was hardly conducive to living the best life God intended. If there was a place to see worldly patterns in action, then Corinth was it. And the Christians living in Corinth struggled to know how to live for Christ as the new creations they'd become when they trusted him as their Savior.

Some of the Corinthian believers had decided to seclude themselves from non-Christians, to separate themselves completely from the pagans living and working around them. Other Corinthian believers refused to let their newfound Christianity change their everyday behavior, and they continued to live just as their pagan neighbors did. Still others adopted a list of rules to follow in order to determine who was and wasn't part of Christ's body. As a result, many Corinthian Christians were missing out on the best that God had for them.

So the apostle Paul wrote to the church in Corinth to help the believers understand how they should live in a place that was so opposite of their new way of thinking. He gave them some great wisdom that we can still learn from today: "We are therefore Christ's ambassadors, as though God were making his appeal through us" (2 Corinthians 5:20).

A Christian who lives like an ambassador is a person who realizes that God has given her a place in this world to represent the kingdom of heaven. In love, she seeks to advance the kingdom of God by allowing Christ in her life to be an example to those around her. She looks at life in a completely different way because she doesn't represent herself or the world anymore; she represents Jesus Christ.

WHAT IS AN AMBASSADOR?

ambassador 1. a diplomatic agent of the highest rank accredited to a foreign government or sovereign as the resident representative of his or her own government or sovereign or appointed for a special and often temporary diplomatic assignment. 2. an authorized representative or messenger. (www.merriam-webster.com/dictionary/ambassador)

How does this definition of ambassador remind you of the Christian life?

AN AMBASSADOR IS ON A MISSION FAR FROM HOME

[Jesus said:] "My prayer is not that you take them out of the world but that you protect them from the evil one. They are not of this world, even as I am not of it. Sanctify them by the truth; your word is truth. As you sent me into the world, I have sent them into the world." (John 17:15-18)

An ambassador is stationed far from her true home in order to represent the kingdom or country that sent her. She's a stranger in a foreign land. She's left her homeland for a period in order to serve the country she represents. As Christians, we are representatives of our true home—heaven. Under the authority of God and Christ, we've been sent to this world to serve God and serve others.

AN AMBASSADOR DOESN'T REPRESENT HERSELF

For to me, to live is Christ and to die is gain. (Philippians 1:21)

Then Jesus said to his disciples, "If anyone would come after me, he must deny himself and take up his cross and follow me. For whoever wants to save his life will lose it, but whoever loses his life for me will find it." (Matthew 16:24-25)

An ambassador represents the kingdom that sent her. In a sense, the ambassador must die to her own wishes and desires in order to serve her homeland. When living in another country, the ambassador is there for purposes other than her own, and she must submit to the governing authorities from her home country.

First Corinthians 10:31 says, "So whether you eat or drink or whatever you do, do it all for the glory of God." In order to serve the kingdom in the best possible way, an ambassador must make sure that everyone around her knows whom she represents. She may demonstrate her foreign culture in the way she speaks, the flags or emblems she displays, the food she eats, or the customs she practices. An ambassador makes her homeland known to all, representing and making known the directives of her governing authority.

THE DANGER OF BEING AN AMBASSADOR

Being an ambassador isn't an easy job. Ambassadors for Christ are often hated and despised by this world—not to mention by legalistic, secluded, and worldly Christians! But that shouldn't come as too big of a surprise, since Jesus said, "If the world hates you, keep in mind that it hated me first. If you belonged to the world, it would love you as its own. As it is, you do not belong to the world, but I have chosen you out of the world. That is why the world hates you" (John 15:18-19).

• Why might a Christian ambassador face opposition from people in the world?

• Why might a Christian ambassador be ridiculed by secluded and worldly Christians?

• Have you ever been put in a tough place or made fun of because you're a Christian? Describe how that felt.

THE AMBASSADOR HAS A MESSAGE TO DELIVER

An ambassador serves as a spokesperson for the authorities she represents. She says what she's told to say. Christian ambassadors, then, are responsible for communicating God's messages. God reveals to his ambassadors what he wants us to share with others about him.

In Jeremiah 9:23-24, he calls it boasting:

This is what the Lord says: "Let not the wise man boast of his wisdom or the strong man boast of his strength or the rich man boast of his riches, but let him who boasts boast about this: that he understands and knows me, that I am the Lord, who exercises kindness, justice and righteousness on earth, for in these I delight," declares the Lord.

Human nature inspires people to boast about their intelligence, power, appearance, and wealth. But that's not what God says our message in life should be. God wants us to boast about his character. God wants us to spread the word that we have a relationship with God and that God is good.

God has given us, as his ambassadors, some very specific messages to share. For example, Jesus took the punishment for our sins upon himself when he died on the cross. That's good news! There's no longer anything we can be punished for because of what Christ has done for us.

What's more, there's nothing we can do to earn his favor. He simply loves us.

That will come as a pleasant surprise to the people who've spent their lives trying to be "good enough" to be acceptable to God—not to mention the people who've asked for God's forgiveness but are still living with shame and guilt. We have a message of good news to deliver: God really has forgiven you! They also need to know that they can experience a transformation in their lives by following God and becoming a disciple of Jesus Christ. When they do, they'll find that they have purpose in life because they are Christ's ambassadors, too.

DOING WHAT'S RIGHT

I conducted a nationwide survey of Christian students, and I asked them, *What's the most important aspect of a Christian life?* Most of them said it was "doing the right thing" or "being good."

It's true that Jesus told his disciples to seek first his kingdom (the wisdom of heaven) and his righteousness (doing what's right). But sometimes I believe we get the wrong idea about why doing right—or being moral—is so important.

Because Jesus paid for our sins when he died on the cross, we're no longer under the guilt and punishment of sin in our lives. That's why it's written: "Therefore, there is now no condemnation for those who are in Christ Jesus" (Romans 8:1).

Rather than celebrate the fact that they're no longer condemned, many Christians assume a position of moral superiority. They use their morality as a license to pass judgment on other people. How often have you heard people accusing Christians of being judgmental?

Jesus, however, placed an emphasis on treating people justly (rightly)—not judging them. In fact, we're never instructed to judge non-Christians in Scripture! That's the work and privilege of God alone (see 1 Corinthians 5:12-13). However, we *are* instructed in Scripture to do justice and to love mercy.

So why do we do what's right? Think about stop signs for a moment. What if all drivers suddenly decided to ignore stop signs? What would happen? For one thing, there would be a huge increase in traffic accidents. Cars would be wrecked. People would be injured and killed. Countless fights and lawsuits would ensue. Ultimately, relationships would be destroyed.

And that's the key to doing what's right. If we don't, then relationships will be destroyed. God has given us moral standards—and encourages us to do what's right—for the sake of relationships.

Here are a few more examples to consider. When a guy lusts after a girl, he sees her as an object and wants to possess her rather than love her. And by doing so, he wrecks any potential relationship with her. When a person steals, she damages her relationship with the person she steals from. When spouses are unfaithful to each other, they destroy their relationship with their mate.

Why does God instruct kids to obey their parents? He does it to improve the parent-child relationship. Any time we keep our thoughts pure and do what's right—without carrying it over into legalism—we feel better about ourselves, which improves our relationship with ourselves.

Not only do our relationships with others and our self-confidence improve by doing what's right, but our relationship with God gets better as well. Consider the following passages:

> Let those who love the Lord hate evil, for he guards the lives of his faithful ones and delivers them from the hand of the wicked. (Psalm 97:10)

> To fear the Lord is to hate evil; I hate pride and arrogance, evil behavior and perverse speech. (Proverbs 8:13)

> Love must be sincere. Hate what is evil; cling to what is good. (Romans 12:9)

> [Jesus said:] "No servant can serve two masters. Either he will hate the one and love the other, or he will be devoted to the one and despise the other. You cannot serve both God and Money." (Luke 16:13)

If anyone says, "I love God," yet hates his brother, he is a liar. For anyone who does not love his brother, whom he has seen, cannot love God, whom he has not seen. (1 John 4:20)

[God said:] "You have loved righteousness and hated wickedness; therefore God, your God, has set you above your companions by anointing you with the oil of joy." (Hebrews 1:9)

Remember, morality—doing what's right according to God's Word—isn't a tool for gaining God's favor or making yourself look better than other people. Morality is a path to meaningful relationships. By doing what's right, you can impact the lives of others in a positive way. And you can represent your homeland in a way that brings glory to the one who sent you.

CHAPTER 3

UNBURDENED

GETTING RID OF THINGS THAT
KEEP US FROM GROWING

For the past several years, I've hosted weekly small group meetings in my home. The meetings offer a place where teenagers can come for fellowship, accountability, Bible study, and prayer. Every year when we start up again in the fall, we see new faces and watch relationships begin. After several weeks of getting to know each other, people start to open up—sometimes about their most intimate experiences and challenges.

That developing bond is an awesome thing to see because it means the group is starting to trust one another. And that trust allows us to pray and support one another during the week. I hope you have a group like ours in your church community.

One night, a boy in our group admitted that he was having a hard time growing closer to God because he was struggling with sexual lust. As a group, we talked through his struggle, and we soon discovered that he wasn't alone—others were having trouble with lust, too. Then other group members began to share about the issues that were keeping them from growing closer to God. As you might imagine, it was a big night for our group! We all prayed for each other and committed to hold each other accountable for those actions that were keeping us from growing in Christ.

At the end of the evening, one student said, "Wow, I thought I was the only one having trouble getting closer to God. Sharing has motivated me to get rid of this, and I think I have others around me who can help." And while the change in his life didn't happen instantly, this young man made huge progress as the weeks continued.

As we mature in life, we'll often face obstacles that keep us from being molded into the people God wants us to be. You may be struggling with one (or more) of those obstacles now.

Let's take a look at what Scripture teaches about overcoming obstacles to our spiritual growth. Our first stop is in the book of 2 Timothy, where Paul uses the following words to encourage Timothy, a young man whom God was shaping to be useful to him:

In a large house there are articles not only of gold and silver, but also of wood and clay; some are for noble purposes and some for ignoble. If a man cleanses himself from the latter, he will be an instrument for noble purposes, made holy, useful to the Master and prepared to do any good work. Flee the evil desires of youth, and pursue righteousness, faith, love and peace, along with those who call on the Lord out of a pure heart. (2 Timothy 2:20-22)

I'd like to be used for noble purposes. How about you? In order to do that, though, we need to get rid of the hindrances that keep us from maturing.

Here are some specific steps we can take to overcome obstacles and clear the path for God to use us in amazing ways.

STEP 1: IDENTIFY THE OBSTACLE

Many Christians aren't aware of how their habits and attitudes affect their Christian growth. That's why it's important to take an honest look at yourself to see what issues might be preventing you from growing in Christ. To put it in biblical terms, what do you need to "flee" from?

I asked my friends on MySpace to help me come up with a list. Here are some things that keep them from growing in Christ. I should point out that just because something appears on the list, that doesn't necessarily mean it's "evil"—just that it's a hindrance to some people.

Circle any of the following items that may be affecting you:

Smoking

Doing drugs

Drinking alcohol

Eating too much

Not eating enough

Blaming others when things go wrong

Believing you're always right

Driving recklessly

Being a hothead

Making sarcastic remarks

Cutting yourself

Spending your money unwisely

Daydreaming

Laziness

Avoiding people

Looking at pornography

Spending too much time on the Internet

Doing things sexually outside of marriage

Being obnoxious

Lying

Bragging

Gossiping

Being too concerned about your looks

Flirting to get attention

Procrastinating

Using profanity

Watching too much television

Remember, if it's slowing down your spiritual growth, then it's a hindrance. Why wouldn't you get rid of it?

My friend is a competitive swimmer, and he shaves his legs because he feels the leg hair slows him down in the water. To say it another way, his leg hair is a hindrance to his development as a swimmer, so he gets rid of it. We need to do the same thing with our spiritual hindrances.

The book of Hebrews explains it this way: "Therefore, since we are surrounded by such a great cloud of witnesses, let us throw off everything that hinders and the sin that so easily entangles, and let us run with perseverance the race marked out for us" (Hebrews 12:1).

What's keeping you from maturing? How can you improve your relationship with Christ by getting rid of a hindering habit? How can you speed your growth as a Christian by changing an attitude? Once you've honestly answered those questions, you can move on to the next step.

STEP 2: CREATE A PLAN TO BREAK THE BAD HABIT

God takes our bad habits *very* seriously. So much so that Jesus said this:

> If your right eye causes you to sin, gouge it out and throw it away. It is better for you to lose one part of your body than for your whole body to be thrown into hell. And if your right hand causes you to sin, cut it off and throw it away. It is better for you to lose one part of your body than for your whole body to go into hell. (Matthew 5:29-30)

Jesus isn't telling us to mutilate our bodies. He's making an important spiritual point. He's instructing us to take whatever steps are necessary to get rid of the things that cause us to be less than who God made us to be.

Jesus is telling us to wage war on our sin nature, which is the cause of our spiritual struggles. The apostle Paul describes the struggle this way: "For the sinful nature desires what is contrary to the Spirit, and the Spirit what is contrary to the sinful nature. They are in conflict with each other, so that you do not do what you want" (Galatians 5:17).

When I was in middle school, I had a very mean PE teacher. If I could show you a picture of me in seventh grade, you'd see a fairly cute but scrawny wisp of a boy. I couldn't grip a football to save my life. Instead, I had to balance it on my palm and throw it like a shot put toward the receiver. I didn't know—or care—much about sports, which made my situation with my PE teacher even worse.

I couldn't do pull-ups. So for my physical education test, I had to hang from the pull-up bar for 30 seconds. The coach made fun of me, and I was the one he always called on for demonstrations (probably because, out of respect for authority, I never said anything about his mistreatment). I even let him twist me into a pretzel during our wrestling unit, while the rest of the class laughed. Fortunately, I had okay self-esteem, but it sure took a beating during his class.

Many years later, I ran into my old PE teacher while I was doing some Christmas shopping at the mall. He didn't recognize me, but let's say he did. "Matlock!" he would shout. "Drop down and give me 30!" If I were to drop down right there in the mall and do 30 push-ups for that man, wouldn't you believe I was crazy? Of course you would! I was no longer in his PE class; he was no longer my teacher. *He had no authority over me!*

The same is true with our sin nature. It may still hang around and try to tell us what to do, but we're no longer under its authority. Because Jesus died for us, we don't have to obey our sin nature's cruel ways.

Romans 6:11-14 reminds us of this:

> In the same way, count yourselves
> dead to sin but alive to God in Christ
> Jesus. Therefore do not let sin reign
> in your mortal body so that you obey
> its evil desires. Do not offer the parts
> of your body to sin, as instruments
> of wickedness, but rather offer
> yourselves to God, as those who have
> been brought from death to life; and
> offer the parts of your body to him as
> instruments of righteousness. For sin
> shall not be your master, because you
> are not under law, but under grace.

Jesus released sin's hold on us. And God
promises that he won't allow us to face
temptations that are too intense for us
to overcome. That's wonderful news, of
course. But it puts the responsibility
and accountability for our decisions
and actions squarely on our shoulders.
Excuses such as "I couldn't help

myself!" or "The devil made me do it!" just won't hold up.

I worked with a student who was having trouble staying sexually pure in his relationship with his girlfriend. One day he came up to me and reported that his grandmother had told him that his family just has really strong sex drives and that he shouldn't be too concerned about it. (I would have loved to listen in on that conversation!) I have news for Grandma: Many people have strong sex drives, but we can't use that as an excuse for sexual sin! Remember, God has given us the power to overcome temptations.

Look at Paul's words in 1 Corinthians 10:13—"No temptation has seized you except what is common to man. And God is faithful; he will not let you be tempted beyond what you can bear. But when you are tempted, he will also provide a way out so that you can stand up under it."

What we need to do is look for The Way Out—the escape route God provides. Here are a few suggestions.

REMOVE YOURSELF FROM TEMPTING SITUATIONS

If you were an alcoholic, then it wouldn't be wise for you to take a job at a liquor store. Likewise, if you struggle with a certain area of temptation, then you can save yourself a lot of problems simply by staying away from environments in which that temptation occurs.

In the book of Proverbs, King Solomon offered counsel to his sons regarding prostitutes and adulterous women who might tempt them. Here's what he said: "Now then, my sons, listen to me; do not turn aside from what I say. Keep to a path far from her, do not go near the door of her house, lest you give your best strength to others and your years to one who is cruel" (Proverbs 5:7-9). Notice that Solomon is trying to help his sons experience a fulfilling life by urging them not to waste it. Solomon wanted the best for his sons, even though it may seem to some people that he was just trying to rob them of some fun.

People often accuse God of trying to prevent us from having fun, too. But that isn't God's motivation. God wants us to experience healthy relationships because, in the end, they're what matter most.

What are some ways you can avoid tempting situations? What kind of commitments would that require? Are there certain people who negatively influence you more than you positively influence them? If so, what can you do to change that dynamic?

Sometimes the best thing we can do is *run* (literally) from a tempting situation. Rather than trying to battle with certain temptations, we need to flee their sphere of influence.

Unfortunately, not all temptations are easily avoided. So what do we do then?

FIND PEOPLE TO RUN TO FOR HELP

Running *from* tempting situations can make doing the right thing easier. But we also need someone to run *to* when things get intense. Some problems are far too difficult and complex for us to overcome on our own. We need the input of other people. We also need people to look out for us when we struggle.

The book of James encourages us to share our struggles and sins with one another and to pray for each other: "Therefore confess your sins to each other and pray for each other so that you may be healed. The prayer of a righteous man is powerful and effective" (James 5:16).

The book of Ecclesiastes talks about the benefit of having a true friend in times of trouble: "If one falls down, his friend can help him up. But pity the man who falls and has no one to help him up! Also, if two lie down together, they will keep warm. But how can one keep warm alone? Though one may be overpowered, two can defend themselves. A cord of three strands is not quickly broken" (Ecclesiastes 4:10-12).

Can you think of at least three dependable and mature Christians you could turn to when you struggle with temptation?

DRAW NEAR TO GOD, AND HE WILL LIFT YOU UP
When we face temptation, we should run not only to other people, but also to God. The book of James puts it this way:

> But he gives us more grace. That is why Scripture says: "God opposes the proud but gives grace to the humble." Submit yourselves, then, to God. Resist the devil, and he will flee from you. Come near to God and he will come near to you. Wash your

hands, you sinners, and purify your hearts, you double-minded. Grieve, mourn and wail. Change your laughter to mourning and your joy to gloom. Humble yourselves before the Lord, and he will lift you up. (James 4:6-10)

If we don't experience the nearness of God, then it's because we've strayed away from him. Because of our sin nature, we have a tendency to become distracted by other things and lose sight of the direction in which God intends for us to go.

The power of the Holy Spirit—who lives in all of us who have trusted in Christ—enables us to resist the temptations of the flesh. The problem is that we often fail to recognize—or to seek—God's power when we face those temptations. According to God's Word, that's a waste of an extremely valuable resource: "So I say, live by the Spirit, and you will not gratify the desires of the sinful nature" (Galatians 5:16).

And when we draw near to God we need to ask for his help.

This is the confidence we have in approaching God: that if we ask anything according to his will, he hears us. (1 John 5:14)

> For this reason I kneel before the Father, from whom his whole family in heaven and on earth derives its name. I pray that out of his glorious riches he may strengthen you with power through his Spirit in your inner being. (Ephesians 3:14-16)

What are some things that take your mind off God? Why do those things have the power to distract you? What can you do to lessen their power? What specific steps can you take to stay close to God during times of temptation?

STEP 3: DEVELOP NEW, HEALTHY HABITS

Getting rid of your old habits is only one step in the battle against temptation. As the old saying goes, nature abhors a vacuum. If you don't fill the space that the old habit occupied—and do so with something healthy and positive—then you can bet another bad habit will fill it for you.

The process won't be easy. Unlike bad habits, which are surprisingly easy to develop, developing good habits requires discipline and hard work. The apostle Paul used a physical training analogy to describe the process:

> Therefore I do not run like a man running aimlessly; I do not fight like a man beating the air. No, I beat my body and make it my slave so that after I have preached to others, I myself will not be disqualified for the prize. (1 Corinthians 9:26-27)

Take a quick inventory of your life. What are some things you *aren't* doing right now that you believe could help you grow into the person God wants you to be? Think of one healthy habit that you'd like to begin—something that will help you grow in Christ.

Here are a few ideas to get you started. Can you think of others?

- Set aside a certain amount of time each day to read God's Word

- Spend time in prayer every morning before you start your day

- Volunteer for a regular service project

- Write notes of encouragement to other people

- Start a journal to track your spiritual growth

- Help people in your neighborhood by doing odd jobs

• Join a Bible study

If you're serious about growing in Christ, then you need to understand that certain behaviors can get in the way of your spiritual health. You also need to understand that you can foster your spiritual growth by putting certain healthy habits into action.

And in those times when you fall short, remember this: "If we claim to be without sin, we deceive ourselves and the truth is not in us. If we confess our sins, he is faithful and just and will forgive us our sins and purify us from all unrighteousness" (1 John 1:8-9).

In order to succeed, you must remember this: "I can do everything through him who gives me strength" (Philippians 4:13).

CHAPTER 4

GROWING IN WISDOM
THE ART OF BECOMING
A WISE GUY OR GIRL

Few people wake up in the morning and say to themselves, *I think I'll ruin my life today.* Yet every day, many of us do things that lead to ruin. We make life-altering choices that result in shame, disappointment, and failure. We ignore the good and chase after the bad. We sacrifice the future for the sake of the present. We embrace thrills and ignore consequences—until they catch up with us.

The question is...why?

THE BIGGIES

When it comes to making life choices, most of us have been taught to avoid the "biggies": Don't do drugs. Don't have sex outside of marriage (or at least don't get pregnant). Don't steal. Don't kill another person.

Other biggies will apply when you get older: Don't get divorced. Don't abuse your spouse. Don't be unfaithful in your marriage. Don't fall into debt.

Take a moment to write down some of the biggies you've been taught (even if they're similar to ones I've already mentioned).

I have many friends who've blown it in several of these big areas of life. And one thing they all have in common is that they didn't see their downfall coming. In fact, some of them were even pretty self-righteous and outspoken about *other* people who'd violated one of the biggies. In doing so, they gave the impression that they were better—more moral—than other people and that they were incapable of making a bad choice.

Have you ever heard of a "tipping point"? If not, I'll use the example of a cow to explain it. You don't have to be a farmer to know that you couldn't lift a fully grown cow off the ground. However, you probably could lift a newborn calf.

Now imagine lifting that same calf every day as it grows. The number of days you'd be able to lift the animal would depend on your physical conditioning. At some point, though, the cow would grow just enough from one day to the next that you'd no longer be able to pick it up. That would be the tipping point.

When I took AP physics in high school, my class conducted an experiment with a piece of foil, a bowl of water, and some pennies. (You can try it, too.) The assignment was to make a boat out of the foil and then place pennies on it—one at a time—until the boat sank. At some point the boat would become unable to support another penny and down it went. The point at which that final penny caused the boat to sink was the tipping point—the moment that tips the scale from one state to another.

Usually the tipping point is the result of only a slight change—an extra ounce on the cow, an extra penny on the boat. Once the tipping point is reached, however, the situation goes from stable to dramatically unstable very quickly.

And that brings us back to the topic at hand. Genuine success in life comes not from avoiding the biggies, but from having mastery over the smaller issues that eventually cause one's life to "tip" in the wrong direction.

Many students who are facing dire circumstances seem blindsided by the events in their lives. They don't know what happened! But all of a sudden, they're in trouble—or at least that's how it seemed.

That's where wisdom comes in. Wisdom is concerned with the small, seemingly insignificant aspects of daily living that keep our lives from tipping in the wrong direction.

CHEATER

Let's take a closer look at one biggie in particular—in this case, cheating on a test—to see what smaller issues are related to it.

THE SITUATION

Brad is a good student most of the time. He may not get straight A's, but he has an impressive academic record. This year, though, Brad has not done as well as he has in the past. In fact, there was a very real possibility that he was going to flunk his algebra final.

As you might guess, Brad felt the pressure to do better. So when his friend suggested that Brad sneak in a cheat sheet for the exam, Brad jumped at the idea. During the exam the teacher grew suspicious about Brad's new hat and exposed the cheat sheet on the bill of the cap. As Brad sat in the office and waited for the vice principal, he wondered, How did I get here?

What do you think? What caused Brad to go from impressive student to convicted cheater? Was it the pressure to do well? Was the subject (algebra) too difficult?

Was it the fact that Brad wasn't smart enough to cheat without getting caught?

The following Proverbs are related to Brad's situation. Can you guess how?

"Diligent hands will rule, but laziness ends in slave labor." (Proverbs 12:24)

In the past, Brad was a good student. This year, though, he began to slack off in his studies. He became a little lazier with his work each day until he hit the tipping point and found himself in a failing situation. Suddenly he had to do well on the test in order to get a decent grade in the class. If Brad had been diligent in his studies, then his grade would have been stronger, and he would have been better prepared to take the test—without cheating.

"He who walks with the wise grows wise, but a companion of fools suffers harm." (Proverbs 13:20)

Brad began hanging around a different set of friends. His new friends weren't into school that much. They constantly urged Brad to blow off his studies and have fun with them. Brad's change of companions contributed to his failing grade. His new friends didn't help him grow; they dragged him down.

"The plans of the righteous are just, but the advice of the wicked is deceitful." (Proverbs 12:5)

Brad's new friends weren't concerned about honesty when it came to doing well on the test. Rather than encouraging him to find honest ways to improve his grade, they advised him to do something dishonest.

"Ill-gotten treasures are of no value, but righteousness delivers from death." (Proverbs 10:2)

Somewhere along the way, Brad became more interested in getting an easy grade than in doing what was right. He wanted an easy treasure—one he didn't have to work for. If Brad hadn't been caught cheating, he might have gotten an A on the test, but he wouldn't have had the knowledge that came with studying for it. So ultimately, the A would have had no value.

Brad didn't set out to ruin his academic reputation. But he made several unwise decisions that led to his downfall.

THE DOMAINS OF WISDOM

While battling boredom one summer, I decided to write out Proverbs 10-29, verse by verse, on index cards. Then I arranged the cards in piles according to topic. When I was finished, I had six piles, one relating to each of these topics: speech, self-control, resource management, relationships, seeking counsel, and contentment.

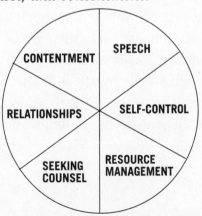

While that may sound like the most boring project in the history of summer vacations, it turned out to be time (extremely) well spent. Over time, those six piles of index cards taught me a lot about wisdom. From them, I learned truths that have kept me from making serious missteps in my life. Now as I share some of the truths I learned, I pray they'll make a difference in your life, too.

SPEECH

The words that come out of our mouths are more important—and revealing—than most people realize. Our words can say just as much about our wisdom—or lack thereof—as our actions do. Jesus told the Pharisees that "out of the overflow of the heart the mouth speaks" (Matthew 12:34). What do your words say about you and your heart?

Here are a few examples of negative speech habits:

- Using profanity and offensive language
- Using humor as a way to keep from getting close to others
- Talking when you should be listening
- Gossiping
- Lying

How many of those habits are a problem for you? How would growing in Christ change those habits? What are some ways you can use your words more wisely?

SELF-CONTROL

The impulses to defend ourselves, feed ourselves, find sexual fulfillment, and satisfy our cravings (whether for fame, possessions, or revenge) are hardwired into our system. They're inescapable.

Our ability to *control* those impulses—to develop a mastery over our bodies instead of being slaves to them—sets us apart in today's me-first culture. It's part of what makes us wise. What's an area of your life in which you feel the need to show more self-control?

Here are some examples of a lack of self-control:

- Losing your temper
- Being unable to handle the changes that happen in life
- Struggling with sexual activity or pornography
- Disrespecting others with your behavior

Do you struggle in any of those areas? How would growing in Christ change those areas of self-control? What are some steps you can take to regain control over your impulses?

RESOURCE MANAGEMENT

We all possess valuable resources, whether it's time, money, talents, or some combination of the three. With those resources comes the responsibility to manage them well. The wise person knows how to maximize his resources for God's purposes, while the unwise person falls into one or more of the following traps:

- Wasting time
- Wasting money
- Wasting talents
- Letting impulsiveness dictate your actions
- Refusing to do his best
- Refusing to serve others

How many of those traps do you fall into? How would growing in Christ change the way you manage your resources? What are some specific ways you can use your time, talents, and money more wisely?

RELATIONSHIPS

God emphasizes the importance of relationships throughout his Word. Wise people have healthy, vibrant, meaningful relationships—both with God and with others. Unwise people have—

- Close friends who influence them negatively
- Too many shallow relationships
- Difficulty being alone
- A tendency to avoid interacting with people
- A habit of disrespecting their parents

How healthy are your relationships? How would growing in Christ affect your attitude toward relationships?

What steps can you take to improve your relationships?

SEEKING COUNSEL

Wise people know how to find good counsel and then actively seek advice from their counselors. In contrast, unwise people—

- Don't know where to turn for quality advice
- Maintain a know-it-all attitude
- Get impatient with others very easily
- Rebel against authorities
- Are too proud to accept advice or help

When you have a problem, to whom do you turn for help? Have you surrounded yourself with wise counselors? How would growing in Christ affect your attitude toward seeking wise counsel?

What are some ways you can use your counselors more wisely?

CONTENTMENT

Wise people are those who've learned to be content with themselves and their circumstances in life. That doesn't mean they don't have goals and dreams or they're not interested in self-improvement. It means they recognize that God has made them who they are and placed them where they are—for a reason.

Here are some signs that a person isn't content with her life:

- Laziness

- Feeling she needs to perform to meet other people's expectations

- Feeling ashamed for something she's done or something that's been done to her

- Habitually blaming other people for her problems
- Feeling desperate
- Believing her dreams have all come crashing down on her
- Envying what other people have

How many of those signs hit close to home with you? How would growing in Christ change your outlook?

In which of these six areas are you currently strong? In which areas are you weak? Remember, the more you grow in Christ, the more you'll improve in all six areas.

AVOIDING FOOLISHNESS

When I turned 15, my dad brought a sign home from work that had been copied and passed around the office. (This was before people had email and

the ability to forward messages online.)
The sign read:

> Teenagers, are you tired of your
> annoying parents?
> Move out, get a job, pay your own bills!
> Do it while you STILL KNOW
> EVERYTHING!

My parents thought the sign was funny, and so did everyone at the office. But I didn't think it was funny. Didn't those grown-ups appreciate the intelligence and superiority of my generation? Apparently not.

It took me a while to understand this, but I eventually figured out that the sooner you recognize that you don't know everything, the sooner you'll mature.

Here are some obstacles that kept me from growing in Christ—some traps I fell into on my way to maturity (assuming that I've now reached maturity, which is debatable). My prayer is that by sharing them with you, I can spare you some of the spiritual growth delays that I experienced.

BELIEVING YOU ARE THE CENTER OF THE UNIVERSE

Plaguing almost all of us at some point in our lives is the idea that we are indeed all that matters in life. The person who is wise—and mature in Christ—lives not just for himself, but considers the welfare of others. When we believe we are all that matters, we seldom reach out to others who are in need.

Here are some clues that you may have "Center of the Universe-itis":

- You do more talking than listening.
- You always try to be first, no matter what the circumstances.

• You experience envy and jealousy when others get the attention you feel you deserve.

BELIEVING YOU KNOW EVERYTHING

Being "wise in [one's] own eyes" is a characteristic of foolishness, according to Proverbs 26:12. And Proverbs 12:15 tells us that "the way of a fool seems right to him, but a wise man listens to advice." When we convince ourselves that we possess all the necessary data, we are bound to run into problems.

You might believe you know everything if—

• You get upset when your opinion is not treated as fact.

• You constantly get mad when your parents try to give you advice.

• You rarely seek others' advice on matters.

- You often find yourself in undesirable circumstances because you listened only to yourself.

BELIEVING YOU CAN DO WHATEVER YOU WANT

Many of us get fooled into believing that our actions impact no one but ourselves; therefore, we conclude, no one has any right to weigh in on the things we do. Rarely is that the case, however. The consequences of one person's actions have a habit of spilling over into other people's lives.

Many recent movies (such as *The Butterfly Effect* and *Crash*) and television shows (such as *Lost* and *Heroes*) have explored the notion of our interconnectedness. Is it possible to save the cheerleader and save the world? Perhaps.

The truth is that our actions have consequences beyond ourselves. Fools believe they can do whatever they want and without considering how other people might be affected. But Proverbs 14:12 warns, "There is a way that seems right to a man, but in the end it leads to death." That's the worst-case scenario for what can happen when you believe you're bulletproof and your actions have no far-reaching consequences.

You might be struggling with this issue if—

- You frequently take physical risks that put you in danger.

- You're often accused of being inconsiderate of other people's feelings.

- "Conflict" seems to be your middle name.

- You run into trouble with people who are in authority over you.

These three beliefs contribute to our foolishness and hinder our growth in Christ. If we want to become wise and grow in the Lord, then we have to choose another path—one called humility.

THE WISDOM OF HUMILITY

If you look back at the three characteristics we just talked about, then you'll see that each one is an attribute of God. God *is* the center of the universe. God *can* do anything he wants. And God *does* know everything. Yet when God came to earth in human flesh as the god-man Jesus, he chose not to make those attributes known. And by making that choice, God set a powerful example for us.

Philippians 2:5-7 offers this instruction: "Your attitude should be the same as that of Christ Jesus: Who, being in very nature God, did not consider equality with God something to be grasped, but made himself nothing, taking the very nature of a servant, being made in human likeness."

Rather than acting like he was the center of the universe, Jesus put the needs of others before his own by serving people. Rather than acting like he knew it all, Jesus frequently asked questions instead of always giving the answers, and he often remained silent when he could have spoken. Instead of acting like he was invincible, Jesus humbled himself by becoming vulnerable to hunger, pain, betrayal, disappointment, and abandonment.

Philippians 2:5 says our attitude should be the same as Jesus'. In other words, we shouldn't consider ourselves superior to others. In fact, we should put others first. Jesus showed us that humility is the key to wisdom and spiritual growth. If we're going to grow in Christ, then we have to do it with a humble spirit.

Humility is important because it helps us draw near to God and receive his grace. James 4:6 warns: "God opposes the proud but gives grace to the humble."

If your family does much traveling by car, then chances are you've gotten lost a time or two. And if your family's anything like mine, when you lost your way, your mom likely suggested to your dad that he stop somewhere to ask for directions. And if your dad's anything like mine, he probably refused, assuring everyone that he knew exactly where he was going. And if your car adventures were anything like ours, you were likely still lost a half-hour later.

Why wouldn't Dad stop to ask for directions?

That's simple: pride. Asking for help would require humbling himself and admitting that he needed help. And that's a tough thing for a lot of dads (and moms and kids and married people without kids and single people) to do.

What's interesting is that no matter how long Dad tried to find his way on his own, in the end he almost always had to ask for directions. How much easier it would have been if he'd just humbled himself the first time!

Humility is a hard thing to learn. But we need to realize there's no in-between when it comes to humility and pride. You can't be "halfway humble." You're either humble or you're proud. And if we take James 4:6 seriously, then we have to understand that when we're proud, we are opponents (adversaries, enemies, foes) of God. Yikes! That's what pride leads to.

Humility, though, is a different story. When we humble ourselves, what happens? We receive grace.

Grace involves receiving something we don't deserve. Salvation is a gift of grace. We don't deserve to be rescued from our sinful life, but God still saves those who trust in his Son—because God loves us.

That reminds me of a time when I was in Florida with my family. My then-infant daughter, Skye, rolled off a bed and screamed so loud that she passed out! We called 911, and the Polk County ambulance arrived in record time to rescue my daughter—who turned out to be just fine. I was glad to receive the help; but a month later, I received a bill from the county for $300 for the ambulance visit. I'm glad the paramedics arrived, but it wasn't an act of grace. I had to pay for that rescue!

That's not the case with God's rescue. God sent his Son to pay the price for our sins with his life. As a result, those who trust in Jesus will spend eternity with God. Jesus paid the price, and we received something we didn't deserve. We received God's grace.

Recognizing God's grace in its various forms in Scripture helps us to stay humble. The more we learn about God's undeserved favor, the less inclined we'll be to claim credit for it: "For it is by grace you have been saved, through faith—and this not from yourselves, it is the gift of God" (Ephesians 2:8).

Grace is also involved when God gives his spiritual gifts to us so we can do God's will—within the church and in the world: "We have different gifts, according to the grace given us" (Romans 12:6).

We live as ambassadors in the world—representatives of God rather than people of the world—through God's grace: "Now this is our boast:

Our conscience testifies that we have conducted ourselves in the world, and especially in our relations with you, in the holiness and sincerity that are from God. We have done so not according to worldly wisdom but according to God's grace" (2 Corinthians 1:12).

When we're in need, grace is what's given to fulfill us and equip us to do every great work: "And God is able to make all grace abound to you, so that in all things at all times, having all that you need, you will abound in every good work" (2 Corinthians 9:8).

When we're in need, we can pray knowing that God's grace is available to us: "Let us then approach the throne of grace with confidence, so that we may receive mercy and find grace to help us in our time of need" (Hebrews 4:16).

Finally, we're encouraged to grow in the grace and knowledge of Jesus: "But grow in the grace and knowledge of our Lord and Savior Jesus Christ. To him be glory both now and forever! Amen" (2 Peter 3:18).

Spiritual growth occurs when we approach life with a humble spirit. In the next chapter, we'll talk about prayer and Scripture reading, which help us humble ourselves before God and receive his grace.

CHAPTER 5

"OUR FATHER..."

THE MYSTERY AND POWER OF PRAYER

As I'm writing this book, Britney Spears is all over the news. You can read about the most intimate details of her life in *People* magazine. You can find hundreds of blogs and Web sites devoted to her. The one thing most of those articles, blogs, and Web sites have in common is that they were created by people who've never met Britney Spears. They've never talked to her. They may do tons of research on her, but they don't *know* Britney.

Many Christians have the same type of relationship with God. They know all about God. They've done lots of research on God. They may have even written blogs, articles, or books about God. But they don't *know* God. They've never even talked to God.

Let's think about that. If you were to stop talking to your best friend, what effect would it have on your friendship?

Is it possible to have a close relationship with someone you never talk to?

If you want to grow in Christ, then you have to build a relationship with him. To build a relationship with Christ, you have to talk to him. And the best way to talk to him is through prayer.

I realize that's easier said than done. Many Christians—myself included—struggle with prayer. So in this chapter, we'll try to ease those struggles by answering some of the most common questions about prayer.

WHAT IS PRAYER?

Prayer is communication with God. Prayer can take many different forms, but it's all about communication. You can pray out loud in a group or pray alone in silence. You can pray on your knees with your head bowed or pray on your feet facing the heavens.

Some people prefer to write out their prayers in a journal. We once did a project here at PlanetWisdom that involved a 24-hour online prayer vigil. Afterward, several students commented that it was easier to communicate with God as they were typing out their prayers than it was during their so-called prayer times.

WHY SHOULD I PRAY?

There are many reasons to pray. Number one is the fact that the Bible says to in Ephesians 6:18 (NET): "With every prayer and petition, pray at all times in the Spirit, and to this end be alert, with all perseverance and requests for all the saints."

I'd say that's pretty good motivation. Prayer gives us a chance to reaffirm our relationship with God. We can ask for forgiveness for our daily sins as we repent of them. We can acknowledge

God as the Creator and our sole Source of Power. We are told to ask God for the things we seek so we can see his powerful hand at work. We can also use prayer to tell God about our day and to ask for his strength and wisdom.

One of the reasons I love reading the Psalms is because they show me how open and honest David's relationship with God was. If David was mad, he let God know it! And if David was joyful, then he let God know that, too. This is perhaps the most important aspect of prayer. Prayer takes our "normal" lives—you know, the times when we aren't at church—and reminds us that God is there also.

WHEN SHOULD I PRAY?

That's easy! *Always.* Remember, prayer is communication with God. How often do you text your friends? That's about half as often as you should pray. I know

that's much easier said than done, but
the New Testament—and the apostle
Paul's books in particular—encourages
us to be in constant communication
with God. Look again at Ephesians
6:18 (NET): "With every prayer and
petition, pray at all times in the Spirit,
and to this end be alert, with all
perseverance and requests for all the
saints."

That doesn't mean we have to walk
around the hallways of our schools
and our homes with our eyes closed as
we mumble under our breath to God.
What Paul is saying is that we should
constantly be aware of our dependence
on God—even during the most mundane
tasks—and be in communication with
God about everything.

WHAT SHOULD I PRAY?

The Bible offers many examples of prayer
that give us some good guidelines as

to when and where and how we should pray. Let's take a look at five of them: adoration and worship, thanksgiving, petition, cry for help, and communion and relationship.

ADORATION AND WORSHIP

> O God, you are my God! I long for you! My soul thirsts for you, my flesh yearns for you, in a dry and parched land where there is no water. Yes, in the sanctuary I have seen you, and witnessed your power and splendor. (Psalm 63:1-2, NET)

This type of prayer involves worshiping and praising God for...being God. If you prefer, you can single out one attribute or aspect of God's nature to focus on, such as his love or power or grace or strength. In modern culture, prayers of adoration often can be found in the form of a song, such as "O Praise Him (All This for Our King)" by the David Crowder Band.

I find that I can offer God prayers of adoration just about anywhere. When I enjoy food or smell a flower or look at the sky, I take a moment to adore God for his amazing creation.

What's something you admire about God? Tell God about it right now!

THANKSGIVING

> Give thanks to the Lord! Call on his name! Make known his accomplishments among the nations! (1 Chronicles 16:8, NET)

> I always thank my God as I remember you in my prayers, because I hear about your faith in the Lord Jesus and your love for all the saints. (Philemon 1:4-5)

This type of prayer involves thanking God for his work in our lives. I love the fact that Paul begins almost every letter with a prayer of thanksgiving for the work of God in the lives of his fellow believers. (You'll find examples of Paul's prayers of thanksgiving in 1 Corinthians 1:4; Ephesians 1:15-16; Philippians 1:3; and Colossians 1:3.)

A prayer of thanksgiving reminds us Christians that the basis of our fellowship is not earthly "coolness," but our spiritual bonds in Christ. Thanksgiving, especially for the spiritual gifts of your fellow Christians, should form the bedrock of your prayer life.

Sadly, we rarely thank God for much of anything. It seems families don't pray before meals anymore, and few of us pray in the school cafeteria or in fast-food restaurants when others may be watching us. It's time to change that trend. God is good; God gives us all things. The *least* we can do is thank God.

What would you like to thank God for right now?

PETITION

> Jabez called out to the God of Israel, "If only you would greatly bless me and expand my territory! May your hand be with me! Keep me from harm so I might not endure pain!" God answered his prayer. (1 Chronicles 4:10, NET)

> Brothers, my heart's desire and prayer to God for the Israelites is that they may be saved. (Romans 10:1)

> Pray also for me, that whenever I open my mouth, words may be given me so that I will fearlessly make known the mystery of the gospel. (Ephesians 6:19)

Petition is a fancy way of saying "asking for stuff." More than half of the prayers found in the Bible are prayers of petition. There's nothing wrong with asking God for things in prayer. Paul encouraged the church in Ephesus to ask God to help Paul become a successful minister. In other places Christians are encouraged to pray for the healing of church members, for peace in the world, and for wisdom on the part of their rulers.

The key to successful petition is making sure that what you ask for is in line with God's character. James 4:2-3 is a particularly helpful passage in this area: "You do not have, because you do not ask. You ask and do not receive, because you ask wrongly, to spend it on your passions" (ESV).

Sometimes we don't *get* because we don't *ask*, and sometimes we don't get because we don't ask for the right things. God isn't a cosmic vending machine.

CRY FOR HELP

Hasten, O God, to save me; O LORD, come quickly to help me. (Psalm 70:1)

The woman came and knelt before him. "Lord, help me!" she said. (Matthew 15:25)

God is always available to us—especially when we face desperate situations. When you break up with your boyfriend or girlfriend...when your parents divorce...when you flunk algebra... when life stinks...cry out to God.

Open up the dam inside you and let your emotions pour out. Don't try to mask your fear or desperation. Tell God exactly what you need. He will answer.

COMMUNION AND RELATIONSHIP

Now it was during this time that Jesus went out to the mountain to pray, and he spent all night in prayer to God. (Luke 6:12, NET)

> Very early in the morning, while it was still dark, Jesus got up, left the house and went off to a solitary place, where he prayed. (Mark 1:35)

> Then I acknowledged my sin to you and did not cover up my iniquity. I said, "I will confess my transgressions to the Lord"—and you forgave the guilt of my sin. (Psalm 32:5)

This type of prayer involves talking to God as though he's not aware of what's going on in your life. Tell God about your day. Share your struggles and successes with him. God is always listening, and he's always ready to answer. Confess your sins to God and open up your life to his scrutiny. Allow God to show you the areas of your life that need work.

Don't assume that communion with a holy and perfect God is always comfortable. The truth is that this type of prayer can be quite uncomfortable at times—especially when God reveals our failings to us. But keep this in mind: Being in a relationship with God is always, *always* where you want to be.

MEDITATING ON SCRIPTURE

Meditating on Scripture is much different from Bible study. Bible study informs your mind; meditation changes your heart and life.

How many of you can remember what you learned last year in math class? What about your history class from two years ago? If you're like me, then you probably don't remember much at all. The reason for this has to do with the way we learn. Most of us study by memorizing facts for a test. When the test is over, we allow those facts to drift away, deep into the recesses of our brains. We then replace them with more immediate information. Gone are algebraic equations and noteworthy dates in American history. In their places are pertinent information on friends, music, and our social calendar.

The same thing can happen to the facts we learn during a Bible study. However, biblical truths are not like scientific formulas. Everything we forget about Scripture makes us less capable of growing in Christ.

Let me put it this way: You don't want to "know" the Bible; you want to make the Bible a part of you. Did you know that people with amnesia—people who can't even remember their own name—can still drive a car? Why? Because driving a car is a skill that's a *part* of them—not something they simply know. They've driven thousands of times. The required skills are written in their nerves, their muscles, and their brains.

That's how we need to learn Scripture. We want it imprinted in our DNA.

Living according to God's Word should come as easily to us as putting a key in the ignition when we get into a car. The Bible refers to it as having Scripture "written on [our] hearts" (see Romans 2:15).

How can we write Scripture that deeply on our hearts? Many Christian teachers and organizations have suggested *memorizing* Bible verses. Frankly, memorizing Bible verses has never worked for me. How many people have the bad effects of alcohol "memorized"? We all know we're more likely to do stupid stuff, to get in wrecks, to get an STD, and to mess up our brains and livers if we drink too much alcohol. But how many people still go out and get drunk every weekend? In that situation, memorization isn't a very effective tool.

Our goal is drawing near to Christ, not passing a Bible trivia exam. So we need to get the truth of God's Word into our hearts and into our guts. We need the Bible so deep inside of us that it affects the way we perceive the whole world.

The way to do that is to meditate on Scripture. *Meditating* on something means to dwell on it, to let it swirl around in your heart and mind. Meditation can be practiced in many different ways. Here are a few ideas to help you get started.

TRADITIONAL MEDITATION

In traditional meditation, you simply pick a passage of Scripture (usually one to three verses) and recite it to yourself slowly and constantly—at least 100 times. For maximum effect, start with passages that deal with your relationship with Christ.

I recently spent a good deal of time meditating on 1 Corinthians 2:12-13—

We have not received the spirit of the world but the Spirit who is from God, that we may understand what God has freely given us. This is what we speak, not in words taught us by human wisdom but in words taught by the Spirit.

In my meditation, I replaced the word *we* with *I*, and I repeated the passage slowly in my mind for a long time. I let the words wash over me: *I have... received...the Spirit who is from God!* That truth is etched into me—in my heart, my bones, my sinews (tendons).

In my line of work, I get lots of questions from teenagers. Sometimes I'm tempted to give them good worldly advice. But as I let this particular verse reverberate through my mind and soul, I came to accept the fact that God's calling for my life is not to give good advice, but to impart spiritual wisdom.

When you get ready to do traditional meditation, turn off your cell phone and television. Find a place where you'll be undisturbed for at least 10 minutes. Pick a verse or two, and then read the passage aloud several times. Repeat it in your head. Let it simmer. Think about what it means in your life.

With traditional meditation, you're trying to be a sponge, absorbing what God's saying to you. If 10 minutes seems like a long time, then start slower—say, with a two-minute meditation—and work your way up to 10 minutes.

MEALTIME MEDITATION
When you pray before a meal, take a single minute to continue to meditate on your chosen verse. Review your day to see if your life has been lining up with what you believe. Think about what's going to happen the rest of the day. Make plans as to how the verse is going to affect that time.

When I was focusing on 1 Corinthians 2:12-13, during my lunchtime meditation I'd review the questions I'd answered that morning to see whether I'd truly offered spiritual wisdom to anyone. Then I'd look over my schedule for the rest of the day to see how I *could* offer spiritual wisdom.

CREATIVE MEDITATION

This one is my favorite. Find a quiet place to sit down with your Bible. Spend a minute reciting a Scripture passage to yourself—out loud. When you're finished, think about how you could represent the truth of that passage to someone else, or how you could remind yourself of that truth.

Then do it.

I happen to love poetry, so I might write a poem that shows how a passage works out in life. You might write a song or a drama, or draw a picture, or

WISDOM ON GROWING IN CHRIST

148

perform a dance, or design a MySpace background, or create a YouTube video or a sculpture. Do whatever you want—as long as you *own* the verse. Try to make it yours. Use your own words and expressions.

Here's a poem I came up with for 1 Corinthians 2:12-13—

> Normal men chase many things:
>
> Money, power, fame.
>
> But they all come to the same
>
> End: Ugly corpses in forgotten graves.
>
> But I have received the spirit of God
>
> All His gifts I claim.
>
> How could I sully that holy name,
>
> By giving advice that makes men slaves?

Do you see how I took the truth of the passage and applied it to my situation?

That's what's great about creative meditation. You just keep poking around at a passage until you can make something that's new and meaningful for you.

As we wrap up this chapter, I urge you to spend quality time with God in prayer and Scripture meditation. I have a friend from Minnesota who speaks with a thick Minnesotan accent. My wife says that when I spend time with him, I start to talk like him. I don't do it on purpose; it's just something that happens. When we spend time with people, we imitate them. It's part of the bonding process.

The same principle applies in our relationship with Christ. The more time we spend with him in prayer and meditation, the more we'll start to imitate him—and grow in him.

CHAPTER 6

WHY DO I NEED CHURCH? I'VE ALREADY GOT A BIBLE

BECOMING A DEPENDENT CHRISTIAN

When I was younger, attending church was something I had to do every Sunday. It was a given: The Matlocks went to church on Sunday. Period. The only thing that could change that was severe, repetitive vomiting. If you threw up only a little, then you still had to go to church.

Don't get me wrong. I didn't mind church that much. There were some great people there—people who genuinely cared for me. Mr. Sedwick, the church caretaker, always had Tic Tacs in his pocket, and he gave me one every time I saw him. He was the "Tic Tac Man." Mr. Sedwick was always at church, and he always served anyone who came around.

Mrs. McGannon, my Sunday school teacher, helped me understand how to follow Jesus. I'll never forget her. Craig Spaulding and Mike Dimmit were two teenagers who took some time with me when I was a kid and made an impact on my life. Craig would teach me magic tricks if I memorized Bible verses, and Mike asked me to pray for him when he went on a mission trip to Mexico. Later in life, I used my knowledge of magic tricks on a mission trip to India. Those two guys planted seeds of inspiration in my life at a young age.

Those are just a few of the people in my church who made a difference in my life. There are so many others, I can't name them all. To this day, many people in my church support our PlanetWisdom ministry financially and through prayer. Those people helped me to see what it means to live for Christ.

I'd like to believe I helped them, too. Mrs. McGannon would always stand up during our Thanksgiving service and share how when she was going through a tough time and wanted to give up teaching, a boy tugged on her dress and told her how much she meant to him. (That boy was me!) But that simple word of affirmation made Mrs. McGannon reconsider her decision—and she was extremely grateful to me for that. In fact, she told that story every year until she left this earth.

There are some great people in our churches—and some really strange ones, too. But isn't that what a family is all about? Everyone has relatives who march to the beat of a different drummer—but we love them anyway. Church is a family, and I hope yours is one that helps you to grow in Christ like mine helped me.

THE PROBLEM OF INDEPENDENCE

Every culture has its strengths and weaknesses. Our culture's great weakness is the false value it places on independence. What's the number one goal of most teenagers? To become independent. The necessity of independence is a myth so intertwined with the American psyche that most of us don't think to question it. We listen to "Miss Independent" by Kelly Clarkson and "Independent" by Webbie. We read historical accounts of solitary men—pioneers—such as Daniel Boone and Davy Crockett. We watch movies and read comic books that feature solitary heroes like Batman, Wolverine, and Lara Croft.

That individualistic, self-sufficient attitude has helped Americans build a successful nation. But it has played havoc with our spiritual growth.

Many Christians in our country believe that attending church is optional—that, if we choose to, we can pursue Christian growth independently, apart from other Christians. That's a dangerous myth. No one who seriously studies the New Testament could ever conclude that church involvement is optional. Every book, every chapter, almost every verse conveys the fact of our *dependence*—both on God and on the church. And any book about growing in Christ that neglects to mention the church is guilty of a capital (fatal) offense.

IMAGES OF THE CHURCH IN THE NEW TESTAMENT

What is the church? Is it a bunch of Christian friends hanging out and talking about God? Is it a building with a steeple and stained glass windows, standing tall in the middle of town? No and no. Those things may be part of the church, but they don't define it.

The concept of the church almost defies definition. Can you define yourself? I can't define myself. Well, the writers of the New Testament never really defined the church, either; but they gave us several metaphors to help us understand it.

THE CHURCH AS A BODY

One of the most beautiful and challenging images of the church in the New Testament is that of a body, with each member serving as a part. The apostle Paul goes into great detail with this metaphor in 1 Corinthians 12:12-31. Take a few moments to read the passage a few times.

> Now you are Christ's body, and each of you is a member of it. (vs. 27, NET)

Paul wrote those words to a deeply divided Christian community—one that's similar to ours today. Christians were jealous of each other's spiritual gifts and financial resources. And they had split into factions over doctrinal beliefs. So Paul introduced the image of the church as a human body. There can be no disunity in a body. Your hand never decides it's going to leave the rest of you. Your heart never stops beating because it's mad at your lungs.

The image of the body highlights two things that Christians struggle with: Interdependence and unity. If the Christian community is a body, then I have to depend on you, and you have to depend on me. In many churches, members are seen as cogs in a machine. If one cog leaves or breaks down, then you simply replace it with a new one. That's a mechanical, modernistic view of the church.

However, Paul uses an organic metaphor instead. Every Christian is a part of a body, with a specific set of functions to fulfill. You and I are not replaceable cogs; we are hearts or livers or toes.

Whatever body part we are, if we aren't serving the community of faith with our lives, then the body as a whole suffers. Let's say that I'm the liver of the body of Christ. If my liver shuts down, then I can't just replace it. My body will soon begin to die. Likewise, if I quit serving the church, then the church will be gravely damaged.

That's true of every member of the church—including YOU. If you don't serve the church, if you choose not to be involved, then your decision will ultimately hurt me and every other Christian. We all lose something valuable when you're not around. The church is hemorrhaging because too many of its members believe their presence is optional. Our church looks more like a disassembled Mr. Potato Head than a living body. Christians fail to see that the church depends on them. We're all interconnected in a deeply spiritual way.

We need to understand that in the body of Christ, the purpose of individual body parts is to serve the *body*, not themselves. The heart pumps blood so the stomach and the muscles and the brain can all do their jobs. Anyone who serves because of what it can do for her is serving for the wrong reason.

We serve the church community with our gifts because that's what's best for everyone. Obviously we'll benefit any time we help the rest of the body, because that body will become a little healthier place for us to live. But we shouldn't serve for our own benefit.

Don't think that you have to have certain gifts in order to serve the church. All Christians have different gifts. I know that Christians are prone to the same vanity as everyone else. To be honest, I'd love to serve the Christian community as a Christian rock star. But that's not my gift. The Christian rock-star gift is not superior to my gift; it's just different. As Paul says, "Not all are apostles, are they?"

(1 Corinthians 12:29, NET).

We tend to overlook people whose gifts and strengths lead them to work with small children or to help with the handyman work around the church. But if we were all eyes, then where would the sense of smell be?

Read 1 Corinthians 12:21-32 again. Reflect on your own gifts and how necessary they are to the functioning of the body of Christ. Don't waste your time and energy being jealous of others' gifts. Throw your life and talent into the fray by serving your brothers and sisters in Christ!

THE CHURCH AS A TEMPLE

Do you not know that you are God's temple and that God's Spirit lives in you? If someone destroys God's temple, God will destroy him. For God's temple is holy, which is what you are. (1 Corinthians 3:16-17,

NET)

It's too bad that Standard English obscures the differences between the singular *you* and the plural *you*. Down here in Texas, we can tell the difference because we use *you* and *y'all*. In Texan, verse 16 would be read: "Don't you know that y'all are God's temple and God's Spirit lives in y'all?" Paul isn't emphasizing the fact that each individual Christian has the spirit of God inside of her—although that is true. Instead, Paul is drawing a picture of the community of faith as a temple of God. When we gather together as a church, God is present in a unique way.

What does it mean that we are "holy"? Despite what many people believe, *holy* does not mean "moral." Why would Paul say the Corinthians are moral when just a few verses earlier (3:3) he said they were behaving like *unsaved* (worldly) people? *Holy* actually means "set apart for God."

The fact that you're a Christian means you're fundamentally different from a non-Christian. You see the world from a different vantage point. That doesn't mean you have to physically set yourself apart and go live in a monastery. Jesus was holiness incarnate, yet he interacted with people, made friends, and even—gasp!—had a good time on occasion.

That's not to say Jesus tried to be "just one of the guys." Jesus never downplayed his "set apart" status. He never set aside his holiness in order to be more accessible. Jesus set the example for everyone who would follow him.

Christians are to be holy, set apart, different. We're called to love others with pureness and without hypocrisy or arrogance. But we're not called to intermingle with people who aren't holy. Why should a Christian never date a non-Christian? Because we are *holy*!

In Corinth there was a temple that housed prostitutes who would have sex with temple visitors as a form of worship. Because the Corinthian Christians knew they were forgiven, they didn't see a problem in sampling the charms of the temple prostitutes—until Paul rebuked them.

You'll notice that Paul *didn't* say, "You know that sleeping around is immoral and wrong, so don't do it," or "You could get an STD, so be safe." Instead, he writes in 1 Corinthians 6:16-17: "Do you not know that anyone who [has sex] with a prostitute is one body with her? For it is said, '*The two will become one flesh.*' But the one united with the Lord is one spirit with him" (NET).

You are united with the Lord God Almighty, the Alpha and Omega, the Beginning and the End. You take God with you wherever you go. So if you have sex with a prostitute or a cheerleader or a football player, then you're taking the God of the Ages with you. You take God with you when you serve in a homeless shelter *and* when you talk about someone behind his back.

That's what it means to be the church. It means we are the holy temple of God, the place where the world can meet the Almighty. Are you living that truth?

THE CHURCH AS A FAMILY

> But to all who have received [Jesus]—those who believe in his name—he has given the right to become God's children—children not born by human parents or by human desire or a husband's decision, but by God. (John 1:12-13, NET)

The teenage years are rife with the struggle to answer the question: *Who am I?* This is true for the Christian teen as well as the non-Christian. You're trying to decide (among other things) what you like, whom you like, and what you want to do with your life.

When a person becomes a Christian, the foundation of her identity is fixed. To be a Christian means to be a part of the family of God. And while that may seem like a self-explanatory statement, the concept of family may be much more involved than you realize.

In twenty-first century America, the family is a vehicle that keeps us safe until we become adults. It's like a protective cocoon. We love our families; but once we become adults, we move on. Many young people spend their teenage years struggling to become independent of their parents. They want to set their own rules and make their own decisions. Teenagers want to be treated like adults, not children.

In first-century Israel, however, the

dynamic was much different. The family wasn't a protective cocoon that sheltered you for a certain period of your life. It was a team (of sorts). Fathers taught sons how to be men like them; mothers taught their daughters how to be women. Sons didn't move out; they added on to their parents' house and moved their wives in. Girls took on a new family when they got married.

Most households had three generations of people living in them. Grandmas, grandpas, aunts, uncles, and cousins all lived under the same roof. Family loyalty was deep and lifelong. Male children considered it an honor to be able to take part in their father's trade. The structure of the family was stable. Divorce was almost unheard of.

In that culture people didn't trust outsiders, so your kin made up the majority of your relationships. Teenagers didn't leave the family to find their identity. Their family *was* their identity. In that culture you wouldn't say, "Hey, I'm Kate. I live in Greenville, Tennessee, and I like cheerleading." You'd say, "I'm Kate, the daughter of Joseph the carpenter."

When we became Christians, we became a part of the family of God. And that's now the most important component of our identity. It's more important than where we were born. It's more important than our gender, our weight, our height, or our skin color. It's more important than how much money we have or what kind of cars we drive. It's more important than our talents, our skills, our likes, and our dislikes.

You and I are first and foremost Christians. Is that how you think of yourself? Or are you still trying to define yourself by other things? You're part of the family of God. You're a child of the King. That's your identity.

Being a part of the family of God also means that we are utterly accepted. Just as God accepted us, members of the church should be unconditionally accepting of each other. Race and socioeconomic status have no part in influencing our relationships in the church. You don't get to be a more favored child of God because you were born in the suburbs or because your parents are missionaries. Being part of a church family means that we should put the good of the family above our own personal good.

A family is a place where you get to live out grace! It's messy and disorganized sometimes. And you won't walk this earth for very long before you get in some sort of fight with one of your brothers or sisters. But you forgive and forget (at least you should) because they're your family and you're stuck with them.

That's how the church should work. The church should be a place where we can *live* forgiveness and grace. For better or worse, as members of Christ's body we're stuck with one another. There's no divorce and no opting out of the family. The church family is built by God. We have no say in who's in and who's out. So live your life in the church with love and compassion.

> But [Jesus] replied to them, "My mother and my brothers are those who hear the word of God and do it." (Luke 8:21, NET)

HOW CAN WE DO COMMUNITY?

As we wrap up this chapter (and this book), let me offer a few tips on how you can experience community within your church.

BUILD RELATIONSHIPS

The church offers you an incredible opportunity to build relationships with other Christians. Take advantage of them!

BUILD RELATIONSHIPS WITH CHRISTIANS WHO ARE OLDER THAN YOU ARE. You may be surprised by what you can learn from their wisdom and experience. Find a few men and women you really admire and start talking with them regularly. Ask them to go out to lunch with you after church. Offer to help out around their house—whatever it takes. Put yourself in a position where you can soak up their knowledge and spirituality.

BUILD RELATIONSHIPS WITH CHRISTIANS YOUR OWN AGE. These friends will be people who walk beside you through life. You can encourage each other because you're going through the same kinds of experiences.

LOOK FOR SOMEONE WHO'S YOUNGER THAN YOU IN THE FAITH WHOM YOU CAN HELP. Especially if you're an older teenager, don't just be a receiver of good things— give back. Use your experience and skills to help others.

WORSHIP

Corporate worship is different from private worship. If you commit yourself to it, then you'll find there's something rejuvenating and fulfilling about worshiping God with a group of people. The church worship service gives us the opportunity to give our offering, partake of the Lord's Supper (communion), and reaffirm our identity as the called-out people of God.

PRAY

It's hard to be mad at the people you're praying with and praying for. Spending time with your community of faith, praying for the needs of your church and its members, as well as the mission of God in the world, grounds your day-to-day life in the reality of spiritual truth. It should also deepen your relationships with others in your church.

CONFESS

This is probably the least favorite biblical command for church communities (see James 5:16). Confession requires two things that scare us: vulnerability and honesty. Yet there's no better way to practice humility and build a more intimate body of Christ than by sharing your failings with one another. Confession offers us a chance to be human at church instead of trying to appear perfect.

Confession also gives us a chance to practice grace and forgiveness with one another. "I'm not perfect, and neither are you. So let's drop the act." Confession should be practiced regularly with a group of Christians you truly trust. Confession should always be coupled with prayer and reaffirmation of loyalty to the goals and standards of the kingdom of God.

SERVE

Getting together as the body of Christ to serve in the community is a great practice. Jesus and his disciples were constantly in the business of helping people. They fed the poor and helped the sick. We should follow in their footsteps.

Service projects can include working in a soup kitchen, building a house with Habitat for Humanity, cleaning up trash at a local park, or helping someone in your church who's having a hard time. Let's live out the command to love our neighbor as ourselves. Service is our chance to show the world what Christianity is really all about.

After [Jesus] sat down, he called the twelve and said to them, "If anyone wants to be first, he must be last of all and servant of all." (Mark 9:35, NET)

In this book we've looked at several areas of life as they're related to growing in Christ. I saved the church for last because it's through our relationships with other believers that we grow the most. Don't make the mistake of believing this book alone will help you. You need to have other Christians in your life.

If you have any questions about what you've read or about new directions in which you'd like to go, then please share them with someone you trust in your church. And let this person help you as you continue to grow in Christ.

It takes wisdom to be a good friend and handle conflict in relationships. This interactive book will help you gain more wisdom and learn to apply it in all your relationships.

Wisdom On...Friends, Dating, and Relationships
Mark Matlock
RETAIL $9.99
ISBN 978-0-310-27927-3

We all love a good song, movie, or TV show. But not everything out there is good for us. Discover principles to help you gain the wisdom needed to help you make wise choices about the things you allow to entertain you.

Wisdom On...Music, Movies, and Television
Mark Matlock
RETAIL $9.99
ISBN 978-0-310-27931-0

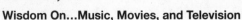

Whether you get along with your parents most of the time, or you seem to always be butting heads, this book can help you understand both sides a little better and improve your relationship.

Wisdom On...Getting Along with Parents
Mark Matlock
RETAIL $9.99
ISBN 978-0-310-27929-7

Making decisions can be as simple as choosing the topping on your pizza or as daunting as choosing your college. Find out how having wisdom can help you with any decision you face.

Wisdom On...Making Good Decisions
Mark Matlock
RETAIL $9.99
ISBN 978-0-310-27926-6

There never seems to be enough time or money. Find the wisdom you need to help you use these resources to better your life and the world around you.

Wisdom On...Time & Money
Mark Matlock
RETAIL $9.99
ISBN 978-0-310-27928-0

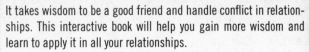

Visit www.invertbooks.com or your local bookstore.